S0-ABC-108

IMAGES
of America

CAMP
PENDLETON

Spanish Frontier Soldier (Cuera) - c. 1790

SPANISH PIKEMAN, 1790S. California's early Spanish heritage dates back to the early 1500s. By the late 1700s, muskets and cannons were in full use by all militaries, but pikemen on horseback were used well into the next century.

ON THE COVER: ASSAULT AMPHIBIOUS VEHICLE APPROACHING WELL DECK. Many amphibious naval vessels have a well-deck in their ships. The rear well-deck door drops, allowing water to flood the well deck and amphibious vehicles to load/unload troops and equipment. (Courtesy of Photographer's Mate 2nd Class Jennifer Swader, USN.)

IMAGES
of America

CAMP
PENDLETON

Thomas O'Hara

ARCADIA

Published by Arcadia Publishing
Charleston SC, Chicago IL, Portsmouth NH, San Francisco CA

Printed in the United States of America

Library of Congress Catalog Card Number: 2005920107

For all general information contact Arcadia Publishing at:
Telephone 843-853-2070
Fax 843-853-0044
E-mail sales@arcadiapublishing.com
For customer service and orders:
Toll-Free 1-888-313-2665

Visit us on the Internet at www.arcadiapublishing.com

Dedicated to all Marines for their sacrifices.

CONTENTS

MAJ. GEN. JOSEPH HENRY PENDLETON. Major General Pendleton pioneered Marine Corps activities in the Southern California area during his 46 years of service from 1878 to 1924. "Uncle Joe," as he would later become known, was commissioned a second lieutenant on July 1, 1884. In 1914, the 4th Marine Regiment was reactivated and Pendleton was ordered to command an expeditionary force to serve as a show of force to quell civil and political unrest in Mexico. At the conclusion of the expedition, Colonel Pendleton and the 4th Marine Regiment landed in San Diego, where they set up camp on North Island. Pendleton immediately recognized the strategic value of San Diego and Southern California to the worldwide deployment of the United States military, based on the area's proximity to the Panama Canal, the Hawaiian Islands, and the Far East. Marine Corps presence in the San Diego area expanded based on Pendleton's vision. With the advent of World War II, one of the busiest military bases in the world was established at Rancho Santa Margarita Las Flores and named after Maj. Gen. Joseph Henry Pendleton.

INTRODUCTION

In 1841, Pio Pico and his brother Andreas received a land grant of 133,441 acres known as Rancho Margarita y Las Flores from Governor Alvarado. This is the land currently known as Camp Pendleton. The Pico brothers sold their shares to their English brother-in-law, John Forster, to pay off their gambling debts. Forster expanded the Ranch House and developed the ranch into a thriving cattle business. Forster died in 1882, and the land was purchase by wealthy cattleman James C. Flood and managed by Richard O'Neill. In the early 1880s, the pair traveled to Texas to purchase several thousand cattle for their rancho. In those days, there were no strict branding laws, so they left the brand that was on the cattle they purchased in place. The "O" topped by a "T" had nothing to do with the O'Neill name. When the Marine Corps acquired the property in 1942, it was given permission to use the brand as the Camp Pendleton logo. The brand was painted on all the vehicles and carved into the tables and chairs at the ranch house when it was briefly used as an officers' club.

The Marine Corps first unfurled its flag in the San Diego area during the Mexican War in 1846. A detachment of Marines from the sloop-of-war Cyane landed to raise the United States and Marine Corps flags on the Old Town Plaza on July 29. Marines played a significant role in the Mexican War, but when the fighting ended, the Corps departed California and did not return for nearly 65 years.

In March 1911, President William Howard Taft dispatched the 4th Provisional Marine Regiment to San Diego in response to civil unrest in Mexico. The Marines landed on North Island establishing Camp Thomas, named after Rear Adm. Chauncey Thomas, USN, commander in chief of the Pacific Fleet. The turmoil in Mexico subsided temporarily and the Marines departed San Diego a second time, only to be called back in 1914 in response to continued Mexican political and civil disorder.

Organized at Puget Sound, Washington, and Mare Island, California, the 4th Marine Regiment, under the command of Col. Joseph H. Pendleton, USMC, embarked on board the USS *South Dakota*, USS *West Virginia*, and USS *Jupiter*, and proceeded to the Gulf of California as a show of force. As stability returned to the Mexican government, the 4th Marine Regiment returned to San Diego and the Marines have remained since.

Between World War I and World War II, the Marine Corps "dug-in" in San Diego. The Corps abandoned its camps on North Island and opened the Marine Barracks at Balboa Park under the command of Colonel Pendleton. In 1921, the Marines moved to Dutch Flats. Early in his command, Colonel Pendleton recognized the strategic significance of San Diego relative to the Panama Canal, the Hawaiian Islands, and the Far East. He began lobbying the commandant of the Marine Corps to upgrade facilities and conditions for Marines in the area, and recommended a permanent Marine Corps base in the San Diego area.

Based on the Japanese threat in the Pacific during the 1930s, and in anticipation of Japanese aggression, the Marine Corps initiated a search for additional military sites in Southern California. In April 1942, the Navy announced the purchase of 132,000 acres that was part of an original land grant—Rancho Santa Margarita y Las Flores. The Marine Corps took possession of 121,387 acres in July 1942, and later added additional acreage to the military installation now known as Marine Corps Base Camp Pendleton. The amount of $4,110,035 was paid for the land to the estate and heirs of the owners under the land grant.

Construction on Marine Corps Base Camp Pendleton began in March of 1942. By late summer of that year, the 9th Marine Regiment marched north from Camp Elliot, east of Miramar, to become the first Marines to occupy the new installation. The base was named for Maj. Gen. Joseph H. Pendleton, USMC, who had pioneered the concept and need for a permanent Marine Corps base in Southern California. On September 25, 1942, Pres. Franklin D. Roosevelt arrived at Camp Pendleton for the official base dedication.

This book is intended to provide a glimpse of the U.S. Marine Corps Base Camp Pendleton. It is not all-inclusive. In 128 pages, the author has attempted to capture as many highlights as possible. Some of the photos included represent the types of training, events, or personnel that are common to Camp Pendleton. The author apologizes in advance for whatever has been excluded or overlooked and for any mistakes. The events of Operation Iraqi Freedom and the occupation in Iraq have been excluded intentionally, out of respect for the Marines and their families who have suffered or sacrificed in the defense of democracy.

One

CAMP PENDLETON HISTORY

On March 10, 1942, the Navy Department announced the purchase of approximately 130,000 acres of land known as Rancho Santa Margarita y Los Flores, located 38 miles north of downtown San Diego. It was earmarked to become the Marine Corps' largest training base on the West Coast.

Construction began almost immediately to build a base to support an enormous influx of Marines to be trained in amphibious warfare, small and large unit maneuvering, tactics, weapons training, and aviation-related training at the dirt airstrip. The base, named after Joseph H. Pendleton, had two primary roads named after two heroes of the battle on Guadalcanal, John Basilone and Alexander Vandegrift. During the base's early days, the famous Marine Corps "Raider Battalions" were formed. Lt. Col. James Roosevelt, son of Pres. Franklin D. Roosevelt, trained one of these battalions at Camp Pendleton during World War II.

Today, Camp Pendleton is one of the busiest bases in the country, occupying 250,000 acres, or nearly 200 square miles of terrain, with 17 miles of shoreline. Over 60,000 military and civilian personnel work aboard the base every day. It is the home of the 1st Marine Expeditionary Force, 1st Marine Division, 1st Force Service Support Group, Marine Aircraft Groups 39, Marine Aircraft Group 46 Detachment A, and a variety of schools, U.S. Navy support units, and many other tenant units and reserve units that make Camp Pendleton a bustling and thriving installation.

"Don Juan" Forster. In 1841, Pio and Andres Pico became the first private owners of Rancho Santa Margarita. In 1863, an Englishmen named John Forster married into the Pico family. Forster paid off the Picos' gambling debts in return for the deed to the ranch. In 1882, Forster's heirs were forced to sell the ranch because of a series of droughts and a new fence law that required surrounding the entire ranch with fencing.

Camp Pendleton Brand/Logo. The Camp Pendleton logo, found on signs around the base, was originally a cattle brand. When James Flood and Richard O'Neill took the reins of Santa Margarita y Las Flores in 1882, they subsequently went to Texas to purchase several thousand head of cattle. The Texas cattle were already branded. Branding laws in those days were either non-existent or non-specific, and the new owners kept the brand.

O'NEILL, BAUMGARTNER, AND FLOOD. In 1882, James Flood purchased the lands currently occupied by Marine Corps Base Camp Pendleton. This picture shows O'Neill (left), his grandson John Baumgartner (center), and James Flood (right) on a wagon during the early days of the ranch.

MULE TEAM ON RANCHO SANTA MARGARITA. Cowboys continued to roam the hills of Rancho Santa Margarita into the 1930s. Here, a group works the ranch using a team of mules and horses.

RANCHO COWBOYS TAKING A BREAK AT THE CHUCKWAGON. Very little had changed on the ranch in the nearly 100 years since its creation. Here, cowboys gather around the chuckwagon to exchange tales and build the camaraderie that would later become a tradition at Camp Pendleton.

ON THE MARCH, 1942. In September 1942, Col. Lemuel Shepherd led the 9th Marines on a four-day march from Camp Elliot, located just east of Miramar, to Rancho Santa Margarita to take over the lands that would become Camp Pendleton. Pres. Franklin D. Roosevelt attended the base dedication.

MAJ. GEN. ALEXANDER VANDEGRIFT. Major General Vandegrift was the commanding general of the 1st Marine Division on Guadalcanal in the Solomon Islands during World War II. In late 1942, during one of the most ferocious battles of any war, U.S. Marines fought Japanese forces for control of the large island. General Vandegrift received the Medal of Honor from President Roosevelt for inspiring leadership during this campaign. The main west-east road through Camp Pendleton is named for Major General Vandegrift.

GUNNERY SERGEANT "MANILA JOHN" BASILONE. Gunnery Sergeant Basilone was the only Marine in World War II to receive both the Medal of Honor and the Navy Cross. In October 1942, on Lunga Ridge overlooking Henderson Field on Guadalcanal, "Manila John" led his Marines against repeated assaults by fanatical Japanese troops. He was credited with at least 38 individual kills, many of them at arm's length with his Colt .45 automatic pistol. The north-south road through Camp Pendleton is named for the heroic Marine.

14

EARLY TENT CAMP. This 1940s tent camp was located near the Camp Pendleton airstrip. During the early development of Camp Pendleton, tent camps were home to all incoming Marines. Marines enjoyed all the comforts of camping out, hiking, marching, and training on and over the Camp Pendleton hills.

BAYONET TRAINING. Marines fighting in the Pacific during World War II established a reputation for hand-to-hand combat and bayonet fighting. Numerous skirmishes involved thousands of enemy soldiers attempting to overrun Marine positions and frequently the bayonet became the last line of defense.

OVER THE SIDE! Climbing over the side of a troop ship; wearing a cumbersome helmet, a full-field transport pack, a fully loaded cartridge belt; carrying a weapon in one hand; and hanging on for dear life with the other hand is a skill that was perfected by Marines during World War II. Here, they train to disembark from ships.

SAYING GOODBYE. Farewells to family and friends during the shipping-out process are among the most difficult phases of Marine life.

16

BATTLE FOR TARAWA. Marines "island hopped" across the Pacific during World War II, giving new meaning to the adage "Any climb or place." Some of the most ferocious fighting in the history of warfare took place on these islands, and individual Marines always emerged as victors. But a high price was often paid, such as the great number of casualties that were sustained at Tarawa in the Gilbert Islands.

BATTLE FOR PELELIU. This moment in time shows Marines on top of a disabled Amtrac, where someone has inscribed "The Bloody Trail," capturing a moment of incredible bravery and courage. With dead and wounded everywhere, and in the midst of this intense battle in the Palau Islands (now known as the Belau Islands in the far western group of the Caroline Islands), the Marines on the Amtrac send fire down range while comrades take a break.

IWO JIMA FLAG RAISING. This iconic photo practically stands for the phrase "U.S. victory." It depicts Marines on Mount Suribachi, the high ground on Iwo Jima, and has been interpreted many ways by many authors. For many Marines, the photo represents the ultimate achievement and the ultimate sacrifice paid in full by the few.

WOMEN RESERVES AT CAMP PENDLETON. Female Marines, also known as Women Reserves, are seen here taking the oath of the Marine Corps. They first entered the Corps toward the end of World War I. During World War II their numbers swelled, and they proudly and proficiently served in a variety of capacities. Women Reserves arrived at Camp Pendleton in 1943 during the height of World War II. Women's uniforms in the early days of World War II were usually modified men's uniforms.

WOMEN MARINES WORKING ON VEHICLE. Women Reserves during World War II filled many key billets, freeing male Marines for duty in combat zones. The women's service and dedication to duty often goes unheralded, but their accomplishments are part of the record.

CURTISS R5C COMMANDO. The Commando was one of many aircraft flying to and from the Camp Pendleton airfield, performing training and delivering troops and supplies. Designed to carry 50 troops or 33 litter patients, the aircraft could also carry up to 10,000 pounds of cargo. Marine transport squadrons (VMRs) flew the R5C. Cruising speed was 173 miles per hour and service ceiling was 24,500 feet.

SBD Dauntless Dive Bomber. The Dauntless was another World War II workhorse that flew to and from the Camp Pendleton airstrip and also was staged at Camp Pendleton during and after World War II. The most famous dive-bomber of World War II, the SBD helped American forces win the Battle of Midway only six months after the Japanese attacked Pearl Harbor.

F4U Corsair, "Whistling Death." The F4U Corsair is, arguably, the Marine Corps' most famous aircraft. Earning distinction during World War II as flown by Maj. Gregory "Pappy" Boyington, the commanding officer of the VMF-214 Blacksheep Squadron, the Corsair swept the skies over the Pacific searching for Japanese aircraft. At high air speeds and in a dive the aircraft emitted a high-pitched whistling noise, striking terror in the hearts of enemy pilots.

MARINES IN CHINA. After World War II, many Marines served in China. The Communist overthrow of the postwar Chinese government set the stage for a later conflict in Korea.

MARINES IN KOREA, EARLY 1950S. In 1950, the U.S. government was in the middle of a five-year dismantling project of the U.S. military as the nation enjoyed the peace dividends earned during World War II. But then the North Koreans suddenly overran and almost annihilated U.S. forces occupying South Korea. Once again the Marine Corps rushed into action.

MARINES IN VIETNAM. The politics of the Vietnam War did not diminish the service of those who bravely fought the war in Vietnam. During the ugliest of times and sometimes the most brutal of conditions, Marines held the flag higher than most and performed without equal.

HAWK BATTERY. The Hawk Surface-to-Air Missile Defense system was developed to provide defense against air attack. The system was placed in service in 1962. The Hawk was a 300-pound, solid propellant, rocket-motorized missile with a range of 23 miles and a ceiling of 30,000 feet. It traveled at supersonic speeds, and the system could fire one missile every three seconds.

Two
CAMP PENDLETON TODAY

The busiest military base in the country provides training facilities for Marines, Navy, and Army personnel as well as numerous civilian agencies. More than 17 miles of coastline, 250,000 acres, and 200 square miles of varying terrain provide many opportunities for Marines to practice and train. Coastal access for amphibious landings, mountain landing zones, lakes, numerous ranges, obstacle and confidence courses, combat towns, and a full-service airfield are among Marine Corps base assets. Centrally located with San Diego to the south and Disneyland to the north, Camp Pendleton is not far from nearly every social, sports, or recreational activity available in Southern California. On any given day a Marine can surf or play golf in the morning on the base, and ski in the afternoon near a Marine Corps lodging facility on Big Bear Mountain.

Encroachment upon Camp Pendleton's borders has always been a threat to the base's ability to maintain a first-rate training facility. Rapid and poorly planned expansion by local communities springing up decades after the base was established has sometimes led to litigation against the base over everything from noise abatement and water rights to helicopter egress routes. The base has a legacy of preserving and maintaining special habitats for endangered species. Camp Pendleton remains an oasis along the rapidly developing California coastline and one of the nation's most productive and modern military bases.

MAIN GATE. The Camp Pendleton Main Gate on Vandegrift Boulevard is about a half mile off the Interstate 5 Freeway and just west of the town of Oceanside. Originally, and prior to completion of Interstate 5, the gate was closer to the I-5 off ramp.

JOE ON THE GO. The modern "full-service" Marine Corps provides a coffee stop just inside the gate. It is a long drive to the Marine Corps Air Station, or Main Side. For those who can't wait, Joe on the Go is perfectly positioned on the inbound lane.

VANDEGRIFT BOULEVARD ALONG YSIDORO FLATS. Along Vandegrift Boulevard, this succession of palm trees marks Ysidoro Flats. Today the flats are a dry riverbed. During the rainy season, the riverbed and wetlands provide a lush habitat for wildlife and fowl.

EL CAMINO REAL HISTORICAL MARKER. In 1769, a Spanish expedition marched north through the present-day lands of Camp Pendleton. The expedition established the string of Franciscan missions along the California coastline. On July 20, 1769, the expedition arrived at the area now known as Camp Pendleton. The historical marker is a bell attached to a shepherd's staff and is one of 450 in place along the 700-mile route between missions. The historical marker marks the route of the original El Camino Real (King's Highway) that connected the 21 California missions.

22 AREA, CHAPPO FLATS. The 22 Area, known as Chappo Flats, is often the busiest place on Camp Pendleton. An industrial area and Camp Pendleton's supply and logistics center, Chappo Flats is the heart of all training and operations.

FIRE HOUSE ENGINE COMPANY NO. 1. One of many fire engine stations on MCB Camp Pendleton, No. 1 is called upon to fight a variety of fires. The firefighters earn their pay for quelling everything from grease fires in the mess halls to wind-driven brush fires in the canyons and on the mountains caused by exploding ordinance. Sometimes, landing zone, or "LZ," fires are caused by hot exhaust from a helicopter or amphibious vehicle. This station is located across from Marine Corps Air Station Camp Pendleton.

24 AREA. The mess hall of the 24 Area is one of many such people-fueling stations located on Camp Pendleton. The history of food service in the international military is a story all by itself, ranging from pillaging the countryside in bygone eras to rations of bread and hardtack, from beans and bacon and "ham and mothers" in C- and K-rations to modern-day backpack MREs (Meals Ready to Eat) and mess halls.

FIREHOUSE ENGINE COMPANY NO. 3. Another firehouse is located at the intersection of Rattlesnake Canyon and Vandegrift Boulevard. Fully outfitted with modern equipment, base firemen are poised to challenge any fire.

MARINE CORPS EXCHANGE , MAIN SIDE. The Marine Corps exchange provides Marines and their dependents with many of the necessities of life plus many of the luxuries. Going to the "PX," centrally located in the Main Side area, after training in the field all week is often the highlight of a Marine's week.

HEADQUARTERS. The commanding general of Marine Corps Base Camp Pendleton presides over the functioning and maintenance of the base's lands, fixed assets, buildings, roads, swimming pools, golf courses, clubs, etc. The headquarters building is where the commanding general's office is located and is the center for all this activity.

MAJ. GEN. J.C. FEGAN MEMORIAL. Maj. Gen. J.C. Fegan served as Camp Pendleton's first commanding general from August 1942 to May 1944. When the 9th Marines marched four days from Camp Elliot to Camp Pendleton, a large greeting and ceremony had been planned. Major General Fegan distinguished himself by being late and by giving, as one observer remembered, "One of the most boring speeches I ever heard."

CHAPEL, MAIN SIDE. During peacetime, Marines are under enormous mental and physical stress from everyday training, expectations, and the demands associated with becoming a Marine. Add to that the complexities of youth, being away from home, family, and friends, and the stream of endearments issuing from friendly staff non-commissioned officers, and the need for a chapel becomes very clear.

COVERED WAGON. The covered wagon on display off Vandegrift Boulevard is a symbol of Camp Pendleton's early Western heritage. From the days of Spanish explorers to those of Mexican vaqueros, from American cowboys to eventually U.S. Marines, Camp Pendleton has had a rich heritage.

FITNESS CENTER, MAIN SIDE. The Main Side fitness center is a modern facility available to Marines and their dependents, and offers a wide range of physical fitness opportunities. Inter-unit competitions, in a variety of sports and track and field events, occur at this facility.

BOWLING CENTER, MAIN SIDE. The bowling and billiard center is a primary recreational center on every military base. These facilities provide an excellent place for Marines to gather after a hard day in the field.

TRAINING CENTER, MAIN SIDE. The training center provides a centrally located facility for a wide variety of training for every Marine MOS (military occupational specialty). Marines are among the best trained military in the world.

SAN LUIS REY OFFICERS' CLUB. The San Luis Rey Officers' Club is one of the most unique clubs in the Marine Corps. In an age of cost cutting and generic modular clubs, which do not provide much ambience, the San Luis Rey Club provides a venue with historic Spanish style and decades of Marine Corps history.

COL. A.C. BOWEN RODEO GROUNDS. Not many bases can boast of having their own rodeo grounds. Near the Camp Pendleton stables and the San Luis Rey gate, the Col. A.C. Bowen Rodeo Grounds present an annual rodeo and sporadic events celebrating the base's western heritage.

SGT. MAJ. W.F. STEPP STABLES. The Camp Pendleton Stables are among the most modern and expansive on any military base. A wide variety of services, rental spaces, and training are available.

CAMP PENDLETON HOBBY SHOP. The hobby shop provides Marines who love to build things and to work with their hands many opportunities to get covered with sawdust, dirt, glue, or paint and to express themselves. The building looks like one of the earlier building endeavors at Camp Pendleton and could be someone's hobby all by itself.

CAMP PENDLETON MARINE MEMORIAL GOLF COURSE. The Memorial Golf Course is known as one of the best courses on any military facility. Located in one of Camp Pendleton's quiet valleys, the course provides the perfect setting for a round of golf on a well-maintained and challenging course. Golf clubs are available, and frequent tournaments provide ample opportunities for lowering one's handicap or simply having fun.

LAKE O'NEILL. This 123-acre reservoir holds 1,300 acre-feet of water. It is used for training and recreation and is a favorite nesting area for migrating birds. For decades, rumors have circulated that catfish the size of a Volkswagen lurk in the lake. Others claim a creature calls the lake home, but these claims are usually made only after happy hour.

LAKE O'NEILL PARK. Adjacent to the lake, the park provides areas for families and Marine units to have parties and barbeques on the lake's shore. Fewer settings provide more scenery and tranquility than this park.

12/14 AREA MESS HALL. Camp Pendleton's enormous size and the wide dispersion of individual units require numerous mess halls. With the possible exception of Sunday brunch, Marines do not have a lot of dining time.

CAMP PENDLETON MUSEUM SYSTEM. The Mechanized Museum at Marine Corps Base Camp Pendleton, located at the intersection of Rattlesnake Canyon Road and Vandegrift Boulevard, is one of three major components of the museum system at Pendleton. The Mechanized Museum, the Amphibious Vehicle Museum at Camp Del Mar, and the Ranch House Museum Complex are all open to visitors.

WORLD WAR II–KOREAN WAR AMPHIBIOUS VEHICLE MUSEUM. The Amphibious Vehicle Museum, located adjacent to the Camp Del Mar boat basin, is maintained by the Assault Amphibious School Battalion. Amphibious vehicles dating to 1942 are on display.

HISTORIC RANCH HOUSE. The ranch house complex includes the chapel, bunkhouse, and ranch house built in the mid-1800s. This was the home of the last Mexican governor of California and later the home of the rancho's owners prior to the Marine Corps' purchase of it in 1942.

STATIC DISPLAY BY 7TH ENGINEER BATTALION MARQUEE. The castle in the 7th Engineer logo is a symbol noting "engineers," and is also used by the U.S. Army. Military engineering exploits may have become most notable in ancient times by the Romans, whose roads, bridges, aqueducts, and fortifications have survived the two millenniums since they were constructed.

CAPTURED ARTILLERY PIECE. A 122-mm, D-74 Soviet artillery piece was captured during the Vietnam War and is on display at Camp Pendleton's Horno Area.

CAPTURED TANKS. A T-55 Soviet tank, BMP-1, and T-62 tank, on the left, are on display across from Marine Corps University. Captured enemy weapons provide students at MCU with the opportunity to study and view firsthand what they many encounter in combat.

AMPHIBIOUS VEHICLE. This static display of captured vehicles and weapons is located by the H&S Battalion of the 1st Force Service Support Group.

RANGE TOWER ALONG BASILONE ROAD. Range towers can be seen all over Camp Pendleton. Range officers and range safety officers monitor live fire sequences to ensure proper procedures are followed and to enhance safety. The officers also keep a lookout for low-flying helicopters and aircraft that stray into "hot" ranges.

DEER PARK. Located along Basilone Road, Deer Park is one of the many parks available to Marines and their families and one of the many natural habitats for Camp Pendleton's wildlife. Wild deer are seen frequently along this stretch of Basilone Road, where the animals feed on green grass and bushes.

Three

THE 1ST MARINE EXPEDITIONARY FORCE, 1ST MARINE DIVISION, AND THE 1ST FORCE SERVICE SUPPORT GROUP

Activated on November 8, 1969, on Okinawa, the 1st Marine Expeditionary Force (MEF) relocated to Camp Pendleton in April 1971. The MEF is the command element for the Marine Corps' principle war-fighting organization for large contingencies. The MEF can include one or more infantry divisions, and one or more air wings, and one or more force service support groups depending on the mission. The 1st MEF deployed to the Persian Gulf for Operation Desert Storm in 1990, then for Operation Restore Hope in 1995, and was ordered back to the Middle East in 2003, this time to Iraq.

The 1st Marine Division is the oldest and most decorated division in the Marine Corps. A direct descendant of the Advance Base Brigade that was activated on December 23, 1913, the division was reactivated on February 1, 1941, on board the battleship USS *Texas*. The division fought 15 major engagements during World War I, spearheaded the counter-offensive against the Japanese on Guadalcanal during World War II, led the classic military maneuver at Inchon during the Korean War, and fought its way out of the encirclement at the Chosin Reservoir. From 1966, the division, known as "1st MarDiv," conducted 160 major operations in Vietnam, where it also participated in thousands of minor operations. The division returned to Camp Pendleton in 1971. In 1991, the division fought in Iraq as part of the 1st MEF during Operation Desert Storm, followed by humanitarian duty in Bangladesh and Somalia.

The 1st Force Service Support Group (FSSG) is a multi-faceted combat service support organization providing support for the 1st MEF, 1st MarDiv or Marine Air-Ground Task Force operations. The 1st FSSG provides a variety of support functions, including maintenance, engineers, medical/dental, motor transport, and ordinance equipment, among other activities.

1ST MARINE DIVISION (REIN) FMF, HEADQUARTERS. The 1st MarDiv is composed of the 1st, 5th, 7th, and 11th Marine Regiments and 3rd Assault Amphibious Battalion, 3rd Light Armored Recon Battalion, 1st Combat Engineer Battalion, 1st Tank Battalion, and 1st Recon Battalion. Its primary mission is to execute amphibious and/or ground assault operations. It is supported by Marine aviation units and force service support groups. The division is employed as the ground combat element of the MEF. The 1st Marine Division is the Marine Corps most decorated division. The headquarters building above is where the commanding general and staff conduct daily business and plan for training and contingencies. REIN means reinforcement or additional support and combat units have been added beyond its normal table of organization. FMF means "Fleet Marine Force," which is the combat arm of the USMC.

1ST MARINE DIVISION (REIN) FMF, HEADQUARTERS. The 1st Marine Division has fought in many of the Marine Corps' most famous battles. They made history on Guadalcanal, Peleliu, and Okinawa during World War II. Names like Basilone, Vandegrift, Edson, and Puller emerged from these South Pacific battlefields as legends, setting a standard for bravery and courage that every man aspires to emulate.

11TH MARINES, 1ST MARDIV (REIN) FLEET MARINE FORCE, LAS PULGAS AREA. The 11th Marines consists of a headquarters battery and four artillery battalions. The 11th Marines provides fire support for the division on the battlefield using the M198 Towed Howitzer. The 1/11 and 2/11 units are located at the Las Pulgas Area, the 5/11 is located at Las Flores, and 3/11 is located at Twenty-nine Palms, California.

11TH MARINES CHAPEL. This structure, one of Camp Pendleton's simple but attractive chapels, is located at Las Pulgas.

44

1ST BATTALION, 1ST MARINES, 1ST MARINE DIVISION. The 1/1 is another one of the Marine Corps' oldest and most active units. Dating to the 1930s, the 1/1 has participated in countless conflicts and operations from World War II to Korea, Vietnam to Desert Storm. In 2001, the 1/1 was attached to the 15th Marine Expeditionary Unit for deployment. As an infantry unit the 1/1 Marines train to perform amphibious landings and combat operations from urban warfare to jungle fighting.

1ST MARINE REGIMENT, HEADQUARTERS. The 1st Marine Regiment headquarters displays unit awards in front of the building.

1ST MARINE REGIMENT, HEADQUARTERS COMPANY. Located along Basilone Road in the Horno Area, Headquarters Company 1st Marines supports the regiment in training and combat operations, often deploying to provide that support.

53 Area Obstacle Course. The Marine Corps' standard obstacle course tests every Marine's agility, upper-body strength, and endurance. The quadruple running of the "O" Course, for efficient time, separates the men from the boys. The 20-foot rope climb positioned as the last obstacle is the truth teller, either you have what it takes or you don't.

CONFIDENCE COURSE. The Confidence Course provides a variety of obstacles that involve strength and courage. Climbing tall structures tests every Marine's nerve and builds the confidence needed to perform on the battlefield.

CAMP HORNO AREA CHAPEL. Military chapels are multi-faith facilities providing a range of services to Marines from marriage ceremonies to counseling and social events. The old Spanish-style reflects the base's heritage.

CAMP HORNO AREA QUONSET HUTS. These Quonset huts are some of the buildings on Camp Pendleton that were constructed in the 1940s and are still in use today. Marines are notorious for their frugal ways, and these 60-year-old buildings support that reputation.

1ST FORCE SERVICE SUPPORT GROUP HEADQUARTERS. The 1st FSSG is a multifaceted combat service support organization that provides support for the 1st MEF. It is comprised of Headquarters and Service (H&S) Battalion, 1st Maintenance Battalion, 1st Supply Battalion, 7th Engineer Support Battalion, 1st Transportation Battalion, 1st Dental Battalion, MEU (Marine Expeditionary Unit) Service Support Groups 11, 13, and 15, Combat Service Support Group 1 at Twentynine Palms, California, and CSSG 16 at Yuma, Arizona. H&S Battalion provides military police, communications, postal, and disbursing for the group and FMF.

1st FSSG Headquarters. Unit awards are displayed above the headquarters entry. The 1st FSSG was activated on July 1, 1947, as the 1st Combat Service Group/Service Command Fleet Marine Force at Pearl Harbor, Hawaii, and relocated to Camp Pendleton that same year. The group deployed for the Inchon invasion of Korea in 1950 and supported the 1st MarDiv throughout most of the Korean War. The unit returned to Camp Pendleton in 1953 and remained until 1967, when it deployed to Vietnam. After several name changes the 1st FSSG moniker was attached in 1976. The 1st FSSG also deployed for Desert Storm, as well as for Operation Restore Hope in Somalia.

LAS FLORES AREA. Las Flores is another one of many beautiful areas on Camp Pendleton lands where the Marines have established headquarters, billeting, and training facilities. Overlooking the Pacific Ocean, the site provides a panoramic view and soft summer breezes. It served as a waypoint for travelers between the Spanish missions during the late 1700s and was home to as many as 300 local Indians. Remnants of an adobe that was destroyed by an earthquake and abandoned in the 1840s can be seen, and the spot is a designated historical site.

STATIC DISPLAY TANK, LAS FLORES AREA. This site was also the battleground between Juan Batista Alvarado and Carlos Antonio Cabrillo over the governorship of Alta California.

5TH BATTALION, 11TH MARINES, HEADQUARTERS, LAS FLORES AREA. The 5th Battalion, 11th Marines, uses a 155-mm Howitzer battalion comprised of four firing batteries and a headquarters battery. The primary mission is the direct support of the regiment and division in time of conflict. That support may come in the traditional fashion of artillery support to maneuver forces or by detaching batteries. The weapon of the battalion is the M198 Howitzer, which has a range of 30 kilometers. The command is approximately 800 strong.

5TH BATTALION, 11TH MARINES, PARADE DECK AREA, LAS FLORES AREA. The 11th Marines (artillery) were activated on March 1, 1941, at Guantanamo Bay, Cuba. With the advent of World War II, they went overseas in the summer of 1942. In August, they landed on Guadalcanal and played an important supporting role in the battles of Tenaru and Edson's Ridge.

STATIC DISPLAY ARTILLERY. A 152-mm, Soviet artillery piece, which was captured by Marines during Desert Storm in 1991, is displayed at Las Flores.

CHAPEL, LAS FLORES AREA. Chaplains serving with the Marine Corps are U.S. Navy officers. Serving in combat, they face the same dangers and fears as the Marines they serve, but chaplains are not permitted to carry weapons.

Four
CAMP DEL MAR

Camp Del Mar on Marine Corps Base Camp Pendleton was established to advance training in amphibious operations. The boat basin supports the Amphibious School, Amphibious Vehicle Test Branch, Marine Corps units loading and unloading for amphibious operations, the U.S. Navy practicing ship-to-shore activity, and U.S. Navy SEAL teams practicing shore breaching and reconnaissance operations. The area is also home to many headquarters units and command elements, the U.S. Army Reserve Center, a recreational boating marina, cottages, and camping facilities. Also located at Camp Del Mar is the Amphibious Museum, the Corporal's Course, the Navy's Field Medical School, housing and barracks, and supporting facilities.

Camp Del Mar has a section of beach that is one of the most beautiful and surfer-friendly beaches along the entire California coast. Water sports at Camp Del Mar include sailing, motorized boating, Ski-Doo riding, and wind surfing. Cottages and campgrounds are available through the Marine Corps Community Services organization, which provides beachfront vacation dwellings at extremely reasonable rates. Camp Del Mar is a self-contained base providing Marines and families stationed there with nearly every amenity possible. In addition to superb recreational facilities, the camp has service clubs, exchange facilities, a chapel, gas station, and fitness center. Few military facilities anywhere offer as much as Camp Del Mar.

AMTRAC STATIC DISPLAY. The Amtrac (amphibious tractor) was developed in the 1930s. In 1940, the "landing vehicle, tracked," or LVT-1, was designed by Donald Roebling and produced by the Ford Machinery Corporation. Designed as a supply vehicle, the LVT-1 first saw combat in August 1942 on Guadalcanal. Over the decades since 1942, this amphibious vehicle has proven its worth, and its pioneering concept for amphibious warfare in the 1930s was certainly validated in practice by the Marine Corps.

RECREATIONAL BEACH. The Camp Del Mar beach provides Marines and their families with one of the best, biggest, and most usable beaches on the California coast. Cottages only yards from the water are available with one to three bedrooms, kitchens, and televisions; many also boast barbecues. Campsites and RV sites are also available.

RECREATIONAL BEACH COTTAGES. These cottages are available for rental from the base MCCS (Marine Corps Community Services) department. Reasonably priced, they provide an excellent recreational vacation spot for Marines and their families.

SURF'S UP AT THE RECREATIONAL BEACH. Long swells provide outstanding surfing conditions on Camp Del Mar's beach. In addition to being and excellent place for training, it is also an excellent place for R&R (rest and relaxation).

LIFEGUARD STATION. The Camp Del Mar beach has a full-service lifeguard station that provides on-duty lifeguards and services year round.

1ST MEF HEADQUARTERS BUILDING. Camp Del Mar is home to many headquarters elements. The 1st MEF is one of three expeditionary forces in the Marine Corps. All are located near major naval bases and large airfields, guaranteeing rapid deployment of Marine combat forces worldwide.

3RD ASSAULT AMPHIBIAN BATTALION HEADQUARTERS.

15TH MEU COMMAND ELEMENT. In support of Operation Enduring Freedom, the 15th MEU (Marine Expeditionary Unit) was the first Marine Corps unit on the ground in Afghanistan. They captured an airfield south of Kandahar and established Camp Rhino.

STATIC DISPLAY AMTRAC. This LVT-E1, an early model Amtrac, had a crew of three and could carry 25 fully armed Marines. It had a land speed of 30 miles per hour and a water speed of seven knots. The plow at the front can detonate land mines or break through enemy fortifications.

1ST FSSG, BRIGADE SERVICE SUPPORT GROUP-1. The BSSG-1 maintains a large, new facility on Camp Del Mar. The BSSG-1 supports the 1st FSSG and the 1st MEF. It has an HQ Det (Detachment), MP Det, Engineer Det, TSB Det, Maintenance Det, Supply Det, and Communications Det.

BARRACKS, 1ST MAINTENANCE BATTALION. Life in the barracks is not what it used to be. In the "old Corps," Marines lived in squad bays, showered in group showers, and sat "on-line" in "the head," yelling before flushing to avoid scalding Marines in the shower. These Camp Del Mar barracks overlooking the ocean are broken up into rooms like a dormitory, with private showers and other amenities.

BARRACKS, 3RD LOW-ALTITUDE AIR DEFENSE. The Marine Corps has made enormous strides over the years to improve a Marine's "quality of life" standard. Marines arriving at Camp Pendleton in the 1940s lived in tents and enjoyed real "creature" comforts, while modern bases provide modern facilities.

OFFICERS' CLUB, SHARKY'S. Over the years, more careers have been made or lost in "O" clubs than on the battlefields. The personality of "O" clubs has changed with the times, but they continue to provide Marines and family members with a great place to go for dinner , meetings, or parties.

AMPHIBIOUS ASSAULT VEHICLE PARK. An amphibious vehicle may be one of the most complex vehicles ever constructed. It travels on water and land, and is a weapons platform and transport vehicle.

MARINA. The marina, situated on the south end of the boat basin, is another facility provided by the Marine Corps in support of Marines and their families. Boat rentals and sailing instructions are among the services provided.

Assault Amphibious Vehicle (AAV) Driving (Licensing) Course. Marines driving tracked amphibious assault vehicles must complete a licensing course. There is no better place to complete this training than at the Camp Del Mar beaches with ocean access.

The Hill, AAV Driving (Licensing) Course. "The Hill" on the AAV licensing course provides drivers with a realistic understanding of the AAV's power and all-terrain capabilities.

FITNESS CENTER. Camp Del Mar, in keeping with Marine traditions, provides a modern, fully equipped fitness center for Marines and their families. Weight-lifting contests, boxing, martial arts, and aerobics are among the many activities available.

FIRE HOUSE ENGINE COMPANY 4. This firehouse is strategically located to support the boat basin, housing, and other facilities at Camp Del Mar. The nearest alternate firehouse that would provide emergency services for Marines, their families, and civilians is 15–20 miles away at the air station on Mainside.

CHAPEL. The Del Mar Chapel is located next to the barracks complex, readily available and accessible to Marines who participate in the chapel's religious or social events.

RESERVES AT CAMP PENDLETON. This is a 1947 photo of Marine Corps Reserves displaying the tools of their contemporary trade, including a flame thrower, bazooka, Browning Automatic Rifle (BAR), M1 Garand Rifle, Carbine, and a couple of machine guns. Hundreds of thousands of Marine Reserves have been mobilized at Camp Pendleton, received refresher training, and deployed to the combat zone ready for action.

HMH-769 (HELICOPTER MARINE HEAVY) ROADHOGS IN A CH53E SUPER STALLION. A craft from a Marine Corps Reserve heavy helicopter squadron lands at Camp Pendleton. Reserves are primary users of the services and facilities at Camp Pendleton throughout the year. The U.S. Army has a reserve center at Camp Del Mar and the U.S. Navy Reserves train at the Naval Hospital and the Field Medical School. There are annual reserve training exercises on base and reserves mobilized for duty report to the mobilization center.

HMLA-775 (HELICOPTER MARINE LIGHT ATTACK) COYOTES IN AN AH1 COBRA. HMLA-775, Marine Aircraft Group 46, Detachment A, 4th Marine Aircraft Wing is a reserve unit located at Marine Corps Air Station Camp Pendleton. The attack helicopter squadron flies Cobras and UH-1s, or Bell Iroquois, better known as "Hueys."

HMM-764 (Helicopter Marine Medium) Moonlighters in a CH46 Sea Knight. The HMM-764 Moonlighters are located at Edwards Air Force Base but are part of MAG-46 located at Marine Corps Air Station, Miramar, California. The squadron frequently trains pilots and air crews at Camp Pendleton. This helicopter is practicing external lifts.

4th Light Armored Reconnaissance (LAR) Battalion. The 4th LAR Battalion at Las Flores Area 41 is another example of the reserves training and serving at Camp Pendleton. The Marine Corps acquired light armored vehicles in 1985. They can be configured for a variety of roles including command and control and maintenance/recovery.

SGT. DARRELL S. COLE RESERVE TRAINING CENTER. The Sgt. Darrell S. Cole Reserve Training Center at Camp Las Flores provides another complex for reserve Marines to report for training. Classroom training, administrative and logistical support, medical screening, and command leadership are among the many functions of the reserve center.

2ND BATTALION, 24TH MARINES, 4TH MARINE DIVISION. The 2nd Battalion of the 24th Marines is located in the Camp Horno Area, with access to all of Camp Pendleton's nearby ranges.

INFANTRY TRAINING BATTALION. The School of Infantry (SOI) provides instruction for Marines from entry-level training to advanced leadership training for active duty and reserve Marines. The school offers 15 programs of instruction that are recognized as formal training courses, or MOS (military occupational specialty) courses.

INFANTRY TRAINING BATTALION PARADE DECK. Infantry combat training is physically challenging and a high-risk course of instruction. Marching, running, obstacle courses, small arms training, and firing high-explosive antitank weapons is only part of the curriculum. Marines spend countless hours on parade decks perfecting close order drill and the manual of arms, and performing physical training.

FOX COMPANY, MARINE COMBAT TRAINING BATTALION. The Camp Pendleton Mountains are usually included in hikes up to 25 miles in length. Carrying a full backpack, weapon, and cartridge belt and wearing a Kevlar Helmet test every Marine's endurance and will.

SOI (SCHOOL OF INFANTRY), COMMUNICATIONS BUILDING. The Infantry Training School trains all new Marines graduating from the Marine Corps Recruit Depot in San Diego. New graduates receive intense training in infantry weapons and tactics before assignment to their first units.

SOI, LIGHT ARMORED VEHICLE (LAV) COMPANY. The only school of its type, the LAV Company teaches crewmembers and leaders maneuvering, tactics, and combat operations.

MARINE COMBAT TRAINING BATTALION BUILDING. The battalion trains Marines in the infantry skills necessary to operate in a combat environment. This includes, but is not limited to, weapons qualification, NBC training, a hand grenade course, navigation, tactics, and patrolling.

SOI Command Post. The SOI (School of Infantry) Command Post, located in a Quonset Hut complex, provides a traditional environment for young Marines.

11th Marines Artillery Training School. Artillery men may have received their greatest notoriety under Napoleon, who was a master in the use of artillery. Sending hundreds of rounds down range against multiple targets is a combination of hard work, basic math, and geometry. The 11th Marines Artillery School is a good place to start.

CORPORAL'S COURSE. The Corporal's Course provides young Marines with the essential education and skills to become junior leaders. Techniques of military instruction, military justice, close-order drill, and inspection techniques are some of the subjects taught at the school. Marines graduate with confidence and are highly motivated to carry on the Marine Corps tradition.

CORPORAL'S COURSE. The corporal's course is held in this building at Camp Del Mar. The facility is easily accessible for a variety of physical fitness facilities located on board Camp Del Mar.

EDSON RANGE. This is the primary marksmanship training range complex for the Marine Corps Recruit Depot in San Diego. The range is named after Maj. Gen. Merrit A. "Red Mike" Edson, who gained fame as commanding officer of a Raider Battalion on Guadalcanal in World War II. His 800 Marines defended Lunga Ridge, also known as "Bloody Ridge," against 2,500 Japanese.

ASSAULT AMPHIBIOUS SCHOOL BATTALION. The school is located in the Del Mar boat basin and is the Marine Corps formal school for AAV training. The officer's course is 54 days long and the crewman's course is 45. The school also teaches a maintenance course and a repair course for the AAV. For the reserves, a gunnery course is available. The school trains over 1,000 Marines a year.

MARINE CORPS UNIVERSITY, STAFF NCO ACADEMY. The Staff Non-Commissioned Officers Academy is a professional military education school operating under the umbrella of the Marine Corps University. The Academy provides staff NCOs with educational and leadership training to enhance their ability to assume greater responsibility and perform billets requiring advanced leadership skills.

INSTRUCTIONAL MANAGEMENT SCHOOL (WEST). Located at Camp Las Flores, this school provides courses in administration, curriculum development, and instruction.

PARACHUTE OPERATIONS. Marines train in parachute operations by jumping into the Case Springs area. Case Springs is a mountain plateau located on Camp Pendleton's eastern mountains. During the early 1970s, the Marine Corps stocked the plateau with a small herd of bison to make parachute jumping more interesting.

"RECON" TRAINING ON THE LAKE, 1965. "Recon" Marines train in special operations using special equipment and weapons. Crossing a lake in a raft might not appear unusual until you overload the raft with seven Marines and a whole lot of backpacks, weapons, and ammunition.

COMBAT TOWN. Urban warfare can be among the most difficult and dangerous combat scenarios. Camp Pendleton has several "combat towns" erected to train Marines to be effective in tight, urban warfare situations.

HIGH JUMPING INTO THE POOL. The Marine Corps is amphibious by definition. Jumping into the water is often part of a survival situation and, if done incorrectly, can be a Marine's final jump. Here, Marines learn to jump from a high platform while protecting sensitive body parts and preventing water from rushing up their noses.

COMBAT SWIMMING TRAINING. Not many people are provided the opportunity to swim while wearing all their clothes, including boots, plus a helmet, backpack, and rifle. Marines enjoy this training on a regular basis.

RAPPELLING TOWER. "Any climb or place" is a familiar line in the Corps. Marines often find themselves in mountainous terrain, and traversing it requires special skills. Rappelling down cliff faces is a lot easier than it looks but only with the proper training.

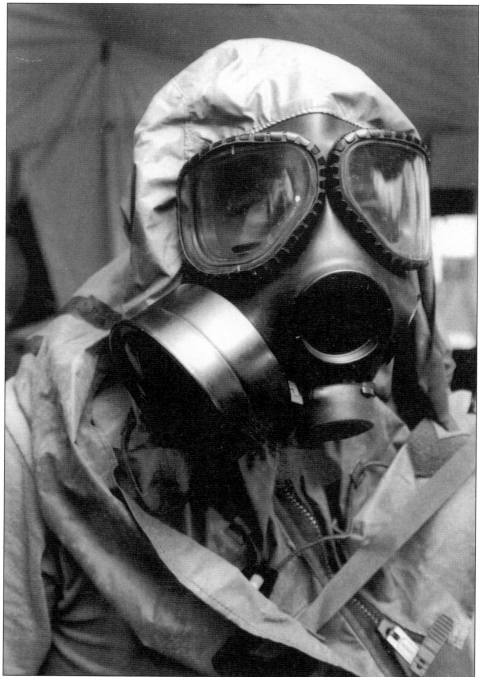

GAS MASK TRAINING. "Name, rank, and serial number" are repeated inside the gas chamber during gas-mask training. Marines learn to put their masks on and clear and test them in seconds. Once inside the gas chamber, they are told by their instructors to remove their gas masks and recite their name, rank, and serial number before they are permitted to exit the chamber. Sucking fumes is, arguably, one of the Corps' least enjoyable training hazards.

Rifle Range, "Lock and Load." In accordance with one of the Marine Corps' "claims to fame," every Marine becomes a "basic rifleman" capable of not only defending himself and his fellow Marines, but also of taking offense against the enemy—with one magazine and only five rounds. The Marines are told to "lock and load," and when the targets are raised for the slow-fire string of fire, coaches are heard repeating "hold 'em and and squeeze 'em." These Marines perfect that skill.

AAV on the Beach. The Assault Amphibious Vehicle is an armored, full-tracked landing vehicle that carries troops from ship to shore. The AAV can also travel inland after breaching the beachhead. The AAV cruises at 25 miles per hour on land and 6 miles per hour in the water with a range of 300 miles. The AAV can carry 21 fully combat-equipped Marines. (Courtesy of USN.)

Approaching Well Deck. Many amphibious naval vessels have a well deck in their ships. The rear well-deck door drops, allowing water to flood the well deck and AAVs and LCAC (Landing Craft Air Cushion) boats to load/unload troops and equipment. (Courtesy of USN.)

TAKING COMBAT POSITIONS. Upon landing on the beach, Marines exit the AAV and take up combat firing positions. (Courtesy of USN.)

HEADING FOR THE BEACH. AAVs make their way through the surf to a beachhead. The AAV's mission is the essence of the Marine Corps' mission. The ability to place combat Marines on the beach is a skill perfected by the Marine Corps since 1775. The Marine Corps was formed in 1775 by an act of Congress and have served on U.S. Navy ships since then, perfecting ship-to-shore assaults.

LIGHT ARMORED VEHICLE (LAV) ON PATROL. During the 1970s, the United States recognized the need for a rapid deployment force. The Marine Corps began testing the LAV in 1980 at Twenty-nine Palms, California. In 1982, the USMC contracted for LAV production, and in May 1985, the Corps began receiving its first LAVs. (Courtesy of USN.)

LAVS ON LINE. During Operation Desert Shield/Storm, LAV units were deployed to Saudi Arabia and operated forward of the 1st MarDiv battle area, providing security and early warning of possible attack. LAVs were involved in the defense of Khafji. (Courtesy of USN.)

LAYING DOWN SMOKE. The LAV has a multi-purpose capability and has proven to be one of the most versatile combat vehicles ever designed. (Courtesy of USN.)

MARINE M1A1 ABRAMS TANK FIRING A SHOT. The main armament of this tank is the 120-mm M256 Smoothbore gun that fires a variety of rounds. The tank commander has a 12.7-mm M2 machine gun, and the loader has a 7.62-mm M240 machine gun. A 7.62-mm M240 machine gun is also mounted coaxially on the right-hand side of the main armament. (Courtesy of USN.)

ANOTHER VIEW OF A TANK. Fighting in the Pacific during World War II involved amphibious assaults and island hopping. There, large tank battles were not common. However, one of the burning images that remains from those campaigns depicts the Marine Corps "Flame Thrower" tanks. In June 1944, the 1st MarDiv on Guadalcanal received its first flame thrower components in preparation for the invasion of Peleliu. The Marines mounted the Mark I Flame Unit on its LVT(4) amphibious tractors. As it turned out, the amphibious tractors did not perform well on the rugged terrain. By the time the Marines landed on Iwo Jima in 1945, the mechanized flame tank had been much improved. On some days the flame tanks, with a 300-gallon tank, spewed up to 10,000 gallons of the thickened fuel upon enemy positions. The battle for Okinawa provided greater opportunities for conventional tanks as well as flame tanks. Okinawa's heavily fortified positions and numerous caves provided ample targets for the mechanized flame throwers. Many enemy positions could not be breached with naval gunfire, close air support, or artillery, but flame-throwing tanks often compromised an enemy position before firing.

TANKS. The U.S. military did not always have the best tanks on the battlefield. During World War II, German tanks were better armored and had greater firepower than the Americans. During the Korean War, U.S. forces fought Soviet tanks, which had other unique advantages. But by the time the Persian Gulf War began, the M1A1 proved itself to be the premier weapon on the battlefield.

ARTILLERY SHOT. Marine artillerymen spend substantial time in the classroom learning the art of placing rounds on target. From the classroom they go to the range to practice their trade. The new 155-mm lightweight Howitzer is intended to be a lighter, more mobile weapon and replace the current M-198 model. (Courtesy of USN.)

ARTILLERYMEN. Artillerymen will argue that their jobs are among the most difficult in the armed services. After tough and extensive training, they are constantly on the move. They are sent to a location on the battlefield where they set up, dig in, and start shooting. Soon the word comes down to relocate, and they do it all over again. A good gun crew can have a gun line set up in two minutes.

ARTILLERY LOADING. Sending rounds down range is the easy part for artillerymen. Gun crews are constantly loading and unloading, hooking up and setting up, digging foxholes, and setting up communication equipment. In addition to all that, they have to perform land navigation, go on security patrols, and camouflage their positions.

MARINE IN FIRING POSITION. The Marine Corps takes pride in training every Marine in marksmanship, as well as the care and maintenance of the M-16 rifle. Cooks, drivers, pilots, and air crew are all proficient, if not highly skilled, marksmen. Marine marksmen's mythical notoriety dates to the late 1700s, when they served in the rigging of sailing ships. Marine marksmen were important in the battle of Chapultepec, near Mexico City, and earned the nickname "Devil Dogs" from the Germans during World War I. The Marine marksmanship reputation continues and the name Marine has become synonymous with warrior and sharpshooter. (Courtesy of USN.)

SNIPER'S VIEW. This is the sort of picture a sniper sees through his scope. Sniper training is extensive and incredibly physically demanding. One of the many weapons used by snipers is the M82A1A .50-caliber rifle, which is effective against equipment-sized targets to 1,800 meters and has a magazine capacity of 10 rounds. It weighs 32.5 pounds and has a replacement cost of around $6,000. (Courtesy of USN.)

SPECIAL OPERATIONS MARINES. Though the days of trench warfare have passed, the need for special operations and related capabilities looms large before military planners. Not all Marines receive special operations training, but those who do are very capable. (Courtesy of USN.)

MANPAD. Here, Marines are depicted firing the "Man-Portable Air Defense Missile." (Courtesy of USN.)

MARINE ON LIGHT ASSAULT RAFT. Marines practice a beach incursion. (Courtesy of USN.)

MARINE FIRING A GATTLING GUN FROM A JEEP. Over the years, the Marine Corps has experimented with a variety of vehicle-mounted weapons to support field operations. Although this configuration is mightily offensive, it does not provide much protection for the shooter or driver.

MARINE FIRING A .50-CALIBER FROM AN FAV. Fast attack vehicles are intended to hit and run but not exchange fire with enemy positions.

HMMWV WITH MARINES AT THE READY. The HMMWV (High Mobility Multipurpose Wheeled Vehicle) replaced the M151 series jeep. Its mission is to provide a light tactical vehicle for a variety of battlefield purposes. This includes troop and cargo carrier, weapons carrier, ambulance, and command/control.

MARINES DEBARKING FROM AN LCU (LANDING CRAFT UTILITY) INTO THE WATER. In any war, it takes troops on the ground closing with the enemy to resolve the issues. These Marines get to the beach "the old-fashioned way."

HMMWV WITH A MISSILE LAUNCHER. The HMMWV is a versatile weapons platform capable of deploying the TOW missile, M-60 machine gun, 50 caliber machine gun, and MK19 grenade launcher. Riders can employ the M-16 Rifle, M249 Saw, M47 Dragon, Javelin, and several anti-tank or anti-personnel land mine packages.

Five

MARINE CORPS
AIR STATION

Construction of Marine Corps Base Camp Pendleton began in March 1942. On September 25, 1942, the area presently known as MCAS Camp Pendleton was designated as an Auxiliary Landing Field to MCAS El Toro, California. A dirt airstrip and meager aviation support facilities supplied training and staging activities for squadrons flying from major airfields like Miramar, El Toro, North Island, and Santa Barbara. SBD Dauntless aircraft, F4U Corsair's, Beech C-45s, Curtiss R5Cs, and Douglass R4D transport aircraft were among the earliest planes landing on Camp Pendleton's dirt airfield. In February 1944, the airfield became an OLF, or "Outlying Air Field," for traffic at Marine Corp Air Facility Gillespie, California. VMO-5, VMO-1, VMF 471, and VMF 323 were among the earliest squadrons to operate at Camp Pendleton during World War II, while MAG-35 began using the field's parking ramp for R4Cs and R4Ds.

On September 1, 1978, the airfield was designated as a Marine Corps Air Facility and became the home of Marine Aircraft Group (MAG) 39. On March 24, 1987, the airfield was upgraded again, becoming a Marine Corps Air Station. The airfield is also called "Munn Field" in honor of Lt. Gen. John C. "Toby" Munn, the first Marine aviator to serve as the commanding general of Marine Corps Base Camp Pendleton.

MCAS Camp Pendleton Patch. MCAS Camp Pendleton is the home of Marine Air Group 39, 3rd Marine Aircraft Wing and Marine Air Group 46 Detachment A, 4th Marine Air Wing. Since the closing of MCAS El Toro and MCAS Tustin in 1998, and the subsequent reassignment of helicopter squadrons to Camp Pendleton, the air space over Camp Pendleton has become much busier than in previous years.

Marine Aircraft Group 39 Patch. MAG-39 stood up at MCAS Camp Pendleton on September 1, 1978. Since then, the MAG has grown significantly and contributed to Marine Corps efforts and operations around the world.

MAJ. GEN. TOBY MUNN AIRFIELD. Camp Pendleton's airfield is called Munn Field after Lt. Gen. John C. "Toby" Munn. Serving in Nicaragua in 1927, after graduating from the Naval Academy, Munn became a Navy aviator in 1931. He saw combat in World War II and Korea and became assistant commandant of the Marine Corps in 1960. He was the first Marine aviator to become the commanding general of MCB Camp Pendleton. Lieutenant General Munn retired in 1964.

EARLY OPERATIONS BUILDING AND CONTROL TOWER. Early operations and control consisted of little more than a phone, a pair of binoculars, and maybe a flashlight. Eventually, a two-way radio was added as well as a navigation beacon. (Courtesy of Flying Leatherneck Aviation Museum [FLAM].)

F4U Corsair. This Corsair is parked in front of the VMO-6 Operations Building. (Courtesy of FLAM.)

OE/OY Bird-Dog/Sentinel Flying Over. The OE/OY observation aircraft flown by Marine units served a critical role in combat operations. Its mission included calling and spotting artillery fire, and directing fighter/ bomber aircraft to close air support locations in support of Marines on the ground. The aircraft could also be equipped with a stretcher for evacuating wounded Marines. (Courtesy of FLAM.)

SENTINEL FLIGHT LINE. Moffet Field is the identifier on the aircraft on the left. (Courtesy of FLAM.)

SENTINEL PARKED ON CAMP PENDLETON BEACH. During the early days of Marine aviation, landing on the beach and catching a few "nays," or digging for clams, was part of the syllabus, but times have changed. (Courtesy of FLAM.)

VMO-2 HANGAR. Since the 1950s and 1960s, many new hangars and facilities have replaced the old hangar pictured here. (Courtesy of FLAM.)

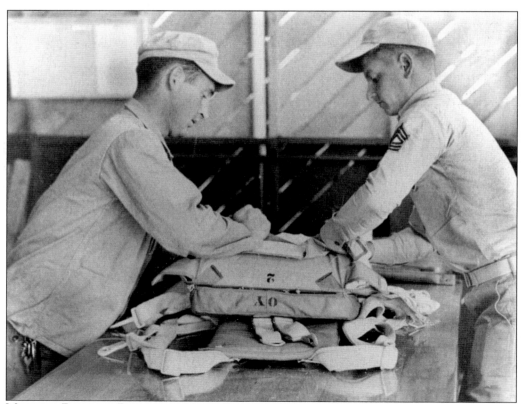

MARINES PACKING PARACHUTES FOR SENTINEL PILOTS. Some would argue that parachute packers are a Marine aviator's best friend. No one would argue that it isn't a skill of life-saving importance. (Courtesy of FLAM.)

SIKORSKY HMR-163 AND HRS/H-19 HELICOPTERS. The Sikorsky HRS/H-19 helicopter was used as the first assault helicopter unit and was deployed to Korea in September 1951. Maximum weight of the HRS was 7,761 pounds flying with a 700-horsepower engine. Maximum speed was 105 miles per hour. (Courtesy of FLAM.)

BELL HTL-4 HELICOPTER. The first models of the HTL-4 were originally flown in December 1945. They were procured by the Navy in 1947 and were used as trainers. Some variations were fitted with pontoons for use off ships, and others were equipped with stretchers for medical evacuation operations. Gross weight was 2,350 pounds, and maximum speed was 100 miles per hour. (Courtesy of FLAM.)

KAMAN HOK-1 HELICOPTER VMO-6. The first HOKs were delivered in 1953. The HOK served as an observation helicopter and also performed medical evacuation missions. The overlapping rotor blades made the HOK very stable in flight. Maximum weight was 5,995 pounds with a maximum speed of 95 miles per hour. (Courtesy of FLAM.)

SIKORSKY HO5S HELICOPTER VMO-2. Initially flown in 1947, the HO5S was procured to replace the HO3S. The HO5S set early airspeed and altitude records, exceeding 130 miles per hour and 21,220 feet. Normal speed for the HO5S was 110 miles per hour. During the Korean War, VMO-6 used the HO5S extremely successfully in the performance of medical evacuations and re-supply and observation missions. (Courtesy of FLAM.)

Sikorsky HR2S/CH37 Mojave with Front Loading Doors Open. The CH37 Mojave first flew in 1953 in response to a Marine Corps need to insert larger numbers of troops in combat zones and to lift heavier loads. The CH37 could carry 26 fully armed combat troops or 11,000 pounds of cargo. The CH37 front-loading doors could also accommodate two jeeps or a 105-mm howitzer. (Courtesy of FLAM.)

Sikorsky HR2S/CH37 Mojave Landing on Road. The CH37 had a five-bladed main rotor system and a four-bladed tail rotor. It was powered by two Pratt & Whitney 2,100-horsepower piston engines and had a cruise air speed of 130 miles per hour. During the Vietnam War, the CH37 was used to extract downed aircraft. It was later replaced by the CH53A/D. (Courtesy of FLAM.)

SIKORSKY HUS/H-34 SEA HORSE FLYING OVER AMTRACS. The H-34 first flew on March 8, 1954, and entered Marine Corps units in 1957. It represented a substantial performance upgrade over the HRS/H-19. It is best known for service in Vietnam in the early 1960s, when at least eight crewmembers received the Navy Cross during Operation SHUFLY. The H-34's maximum weight is 14,000 pounds and maximum air speed is 132 miles per hour. (Courtesy of FLAM.)

SIKORSKY HUS/H-34 SEA HORSE LIFTING A SENTINEL. The H-34 was one of the first helicopters that could lift a substantial external load. (Courtesy of FLAM.)

FLIGHT LINE, CAMP PENDLETON AIRFIELD. The Bell UH-1 Iroquois evolved from a 1955 U.S. Army requirement for a utility helicopter. The initial Army designation was HU-1, which evolved into the famous "Huey" nickname. The UH-1 became one of the most successful airframes in aviation history and continues to be used to this day in many countries around the world. (Courtesy of FLAM.)

MARINES SPIE (SPECIAL PERSONNEL INSERTION/EXTRACTDION) RIGGING. The UH-1 is an incredibly flexible airframe capable of supporting a variety of missions. Here, Marines attach themselves to a special cable and are lifted for insertion into areas where there is no landing zone. The Huey can put them down on top of buildings or anywhere no landing is possible. (Courtesy of FLAM.)

FLYING OVER CAMP PENDLETON RANGES. UH-1s have been firing various weapons packages since the early 1960s. The ranges at Camp Pendleton provide many opportunities for weapons training. The UH-1's maximum speed is 140 miles per hour and its gross weight is 9,000 pounds. (Courtesy of FLAM.)

NORTH AMERICAN OV-10 BRONCO ON FLIGHT LINE. The OV-10 was delivered to VMO-2 in February 1968 and was deployed for combat duty in Vietnam the same year. Designed with compartments behind the cockpits for counter-insurgency "para-ops," or paramilitary operations, Bronco missions also included helicopter escorts, light-armed reconnaissance, and forward air control duties. The rear compartment can also carry cargo or two stretchers. (Courtesy of FLAM.)

BOEING CH46 SEA KNIGHT. The CH46 is easily recognized among helicopters by its tandem rotor head configuration. The design, a descendent of the "Flying Banana," a Sikorsky H-21, has three rotor blades attached to a forward and aft transmission system. Here, Marines exit the helicopter's ramp and slide down a rope making a quick exit from the helo. (Courtesy of FLAM.)

BOEING CH46 SEA KNIGHT LIFTING AN EXTERNAL LOAD. The CH46's first flight was in August 1962, and by the turn of the century, the helicopter had received many upgrades. Maximum speed is 166 miles per hour and maximum gross weight is 23,000 pounds. Here, the CH46 crew practices lifting external loads, which is one of its primary missions. (Courtesy of FLAM.)

CREW CHIEF AT HIS STATION. The helicopter crew chief is a vital and required part of any transport helicopter crew. From this position he gives the pilots clearance when landing in tight landing zones and directions when attempting to pick up or deliver an external load. The crew chief also fires the .50-caliber machine gun and must be qualified on night-vision goggles.

SIKORSKY CH53D SEA STALLION LANDING IN THE SURF. This CH53D performs an emergency landing into the surf along the California coast. The pilot executed a spectacular autorotation and all aboard survived. Mechanics remove the rotor blades and prepare the stricken helicopter to be lifted from the surf by another CH53D. (Courtesy of FLAM.)

Sikorsky CH53E Super Stallion Lifting an Artillery Piece. The CH53E Super Stallion arrived in the Marine Corps inventory in the early 1980s and redefined the meaning of "heavy lift" in helicopter circles. Its maximum gross weight is 73,500 pounds with an external load and maximum speed is 150 miles per hour. The "E" model has seven main rotor blades and three engines. The in-flight refueling probe allows the aircraft to fly long missions to insert or extract troops. (Courtesy of FLAM.)

SIKORSKY CH53E SUPER STALLION LANDING AT CASE SPRINGS. The CH53E is approximately 27 feet longer than the CH53D model. This makes landing in confined landing zones, or LZs, extremely challenging. Here, a crew practices landing at Case Springs in the Camp Pendleton Mountains. (Courtesy of FLAM.)

BELL AH1 COBRAS, EARLY MODELS IN FLIGHT. In 1966, the Department of Defense contracted with Bell Helicopters for 1,100 AH1Gs. The Marine Corps later developed the AH1J and, eventually, the AH1T was created. In 1983, the Marine Corps contracted for 44 AH1W Super Cobras. Currently, a four-bladed Cobra, the AH1Z, is under development. (Courtesy of FLAM.)

COBRA IN FLIGHT. The Cobra has been in service since the 1960s and the Vietnam War. It has seen many upgrades, including improved engines, rotor blades, weapons systems, and avionics. It remains a stalwart and formidable weapons platform.

BELL AV8B HARRIER TAKING OFF FLIGHT DECK. The Harrier concept was particularly well suited to the special combat and expeditionary needs of the Marine Corps. Its mission is to attack and destroy surface and air targets, to escort helicopters, and to provide close air support for ground forces. Maximum speed for the Harrier is 550 miles per hour. It has one 25-mm gun system and can carry six 500-pound bombs or four missiles. Harriers are frequently seen flying off amphibious ships along the Camp Pendleton coast and landing at coastal landing zones. (Courtesy of USN.)

USS *SAIPAN*. Over the years landing platforms for helicopters have grown in size and sophistication. The USS *Saipan* is one of the largest and most sophisticated to date. Its mission is to support amphibious landings from ship to shore with assault troops, cargo, and supplies. It has a well deck that can hold up to seven amphibious vehicles of various sizes. The ship is 820 feet long, with a speed of greater than 30 knots, and can carry more than 50 aircraft. It also carries nearly 1,900 Marine officers and enlisted. (Courtesy of USN.)

AIRCRAFT RESCUE/FIRE FIGHTING/RECOVERY. Crash crew Marines train for those incredibly important and disastrous moments when their skills can mean the difference between life and death.

MARINE WING SUPPORT SQUADRON. MWSS units are a cross between the Seabees and an all-in-one contracting company. They can just about do it all, from building an expeditionary air strip on a tropical island or in the desert, to setting up a water purification station, a medical facility, a portable control tower, and more. MWSS is one of the units that make the Marine Corps "portable."

Six

U.S. NAVY

The U.S. Navy presence on Camp Pendleton is extensive. The Navy supports the Marine Corps in many ways, but the most obvious support comes from the Naval Hospital, the Field Medical Service School, and the Landing Craft Air Cushion (LCAC) facility. The Marine Corps and Camp Pendleton, specifically, are extraordinarily fortunate to have the Naval Hospital located on the base. In addition to providing on-site medical care and a wealth of credentialed practitioners, the hospital is a training hub for active-duty reserve medical personnel, resulting in a dynamic and professional medical facility. Navy corpsmen serving with Fleet Marine Force (FMF) units are among the most respected men and women in any branch of any service. Combining their humanitarian duties with their unparalleled courage often places them in the most dangerous combat scenarios.

The Navy's Field Medical Service School (FMSS), located at Camp Del Mar, provides transition training for Navy corpsman about to serve in the FMF. The FMSS teaches corpsmen how to survive "in the field" with the Marines they support. Corpsmen learn everything from preparing an MRE (Meal-Ready to Eat) to packing a field pack.

Assault Craft Unit-5, located on a Camp Pendleton beach just north of Camp Del Mar, is a state-of-the-art facility that provides the deployment, training, and maintenance of Landing Craft Air Cushion. The unit's purpose is to provide high-speed transfer from ship to shore of personnel, equipment, and supplies to designated coastal sites. The ACU-5 compound spans over 48 acres and has 225,000 square feet of hangar space to support 35 craft and nearly 600 personnel.

U.S. NAVAL HOSPITAL. The Navy Hospital at Camp Pendleton, overlooking Lake O'Neill, provides high-quality health care services to Marines, their families, and retired Marines. The hospital has a 90 percent certified medical staff compared to 82 percent in the civilian community. The hospital has a very busy pharmacy and offers classes to patients and family members to help patients actively participate in their care and recovery.

U.S. NAVAL HOSPITAL MEMORIAL. The U.S. Navy Corpsman Memorial in front of the Navy Hospital is a proud tribute to the heroic contributions made by Navy corpsman serving with the Fleet Marine Force. A small Iwo Jima monument adjacent to the Corpsman Memorial contains actual sand from the Iwo Jima beaches where Marines and corpsman fought and died side by side.

HOSPITAL BARRACKS. The Navy barracks at Naval Hospital Camp Pendleton is situated in a pleasant and shady area adjacent to the hospital.

HOSPITAL HELICOPTER LANDING ZONE. Any Marine injured in the field at Camp Pendleton can rely on an expeditious medical evacuation by helicopter to the Naval Hospital. The hospital landing zone is located behind the hospital for easy access by helicopters and rapid transportation to the emergency room.

FIELD MEDICAL SERVICE SCHOOL (FMSS). The origins of the Field Medical Service School date to the beginning of the Korean War. Navy corpsmen arriving at the school are already trained at Navy boot camps and in medical expertise but are unfamiliar with Marine Corps procedures. The FMSS trains corpsmen to function while serving with Marine Corps combat units.

FMSS OBSTACLE COURSE. The FMSS obstacle course is one of the many types of Marine Corps training that aspiring corpsmen receive while attending the FMSS. In addition to physical fitness, Navy corpsmen must learn the science of "foot care" in order to join Marines on patrols or forced marches.

HOSPITALMAN R.D. DEWERT. Hospitalman R.D. Dewert posthumously received the Medal of Honor for serving as a corpsman in support of the 1st MarDiv during the Korean War in April 1951. While rescuing his wounded Marines on four consecutive occasions during an enemy attack—and ignoring his own wounds—Dewert was mortally wounded by enemy fire. Many great acts of heroism have been performed by corpsman. (Courtesy of USN.)

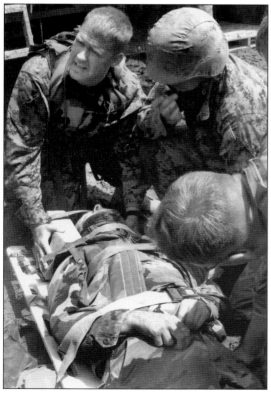

TREATING INJURED MARINES. Modern corpsmen carry on the tradition of caring for injured and wounded Marines. Marines hold combat corpsmen in the highest regard for their heroism and dedication to duty. Few jobs require greater courage. (Courtesy of USN.)

WORLD WAR 1 NURSE AND MARINES. Marines have long heralded the care provided by Navy nurses. The Naval Nurse Corps is as highly regarded by Marines as any branch of the military. (Courtesy of USN.)

MOBILE DENTAL UNIT, 1ST MARINE DIVISION. This mobile dental unit was used during the Korean War and was dedicated to a USN dentalman killed in action on November 7, 1950. (Courtesy of USN.)

CHURCH SERVICES. Navy chaplains are among the most overworked members of the Navy–Marine Corps team. Chaplains assist Marines in dealing with the many stresses associated with training, deployment, and/or combat. Chaplains are available from many religious backgrounds and also perform religious services at the many base chapels.

ASSAULT CRAFT UNIT 5 LOGO. ACU-5 was commissioned in October 1983 in Panama City, Florida, and received its first LCAC in December 1984. Since then the unit has deployed to Okinawa, Desert Storm, and Somalia. The unit has also supported operations and exercises off the Camp Pendleton coast, including firefighting on Santa Catalina Island.

LCAC on Ramp. The LCAC can carry heavy payloads like the M1A1 Abrams tank, the AAV, and LAV. Air cushion technology allows the LCAC to reach 70 percent of the world's coastlines while only 15 percent are accessible by conventional landing craft. The first LCAC was delivered to the Navy in 1984 and became operational in 1986. (Courtesy of USN.)

AAV Loading an LCAC On Board. The LCAC is powered by four gas turbine engines—two for power and two for lift. It is 88 feet long and 47 feet wide, displacing 87.2 tons when light and up to 185 tons fully loaded. The LCAC can accelerate to 47 miles per hour fully loaded. It has a crew of five and has two 12.7-mm machine guns or .50-caliber machine guns and an Mk-19 Mod3 40-mm grenade launcher and an M-60 machine gun. (Courtesy of USN.)

LCAC Unloading Tank. The LCAC generally hovers three feet above the surface when traveling from ship to shore. It has a fuel capacity of 7,130 gallons. By 2001, 91 LCACs have been delivered to the Navy. (Courtesy of USN.)

LCAC Beach Director. During an assault or even a peaceful landing, the beach area can become extremely congested. Tremendous planning goes into receiving supplies and personnel on the beach. Here, a beach landing team member directs LCAC traffic. (Courtesy of USN.)

LAV LOADING AN LCAC ON BOARD. The LCAC has four engines (Allied Signal TF40B Gas Turbines). Two are used for propulsion and two for lift to propel the LCAC three feet above the water, yeilding 16,000 horsepower.

LAV OFF-LOADING AN LCAC. The LCAC displaces up to 185 metric tons fully loaded, and has a range of 200 miles at 40 knots, or 300 miles at 35 knots. It is 47 feet wide and 88 feet long.

Seven

OCEANSIDE

In the early 1870s, the township of San Luis Rey was established and inhabited mostly by English settlers. By 1882, a railroad was built from Los Angeles to San Diego. In 1883, Andrew Jackson Meyers applied for a Homestead Act grant on the Oceanside mesa and was allotted 160 acres. Meyers is recognized as the founder of the city of Oceanside based on his first homestead and the fact that he built the first house on Oceanside property.

In 1888, Oceanside was incorporated with a population of about 1,000. In the late 1910s, the first paved road was built between Los Angeles and San Diego and that accelerated city prosperity. When the government located a Marine base at Santa Margarita y Los Flores, the City of Oceanside turned into a boomtown. By 1950, the population had grown to 20,000 residents. Oceanside's growth has continued, and the population today nears 150,000. Oceanside is and has been home to hundreds of thousands of Marines over the years and has been one of the finest "ports o' call" where a Marine could hope to be stationed.

OCEANSIDE SIGN. This marquee along the Interstate 5 Freeway, just north of the Camp Pendleton exit, announces Camp Pendleton's sister city of Oceanside. Today Oceanside is one of California's most accessible beach cities with one of the Pacific Coast's nicest beaches. For over a half-century, the city has provided Camp Pendleton's thousands of Marines with a pleasant break from rigorous training and often-lonely duty away from home.

OCEANSIDE BEACH. One of the best-maintained and most public-friendly beaches on the entire California coast, Oceanside Beach remains one of the state's best kept secrets.

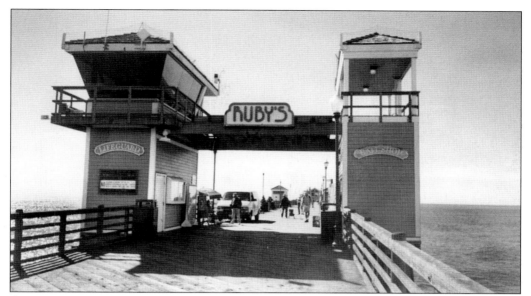

OCEANSIDE WHARF AND RUBY'S. Construction of the first Oceanside Wharf began in May 1888, when the city had a population of 1,000. In 1890, the wharf was destroyed by a storm. In 1893, the second wharf was the first of five that were built at the Third Street location, including the current wharf, which was completed in 1987. Ruby's, located at the end of the wharf, has a location that cannot be beat.

THE 101 CAFÉ. A flashback to the 1950s and 1960s and the Beach Boys, the 101 Café is an Oceanside landmark as well as a popular place to eat.

CALIFORNIA SURF MUSEUM. The California Surf Museum has one of the world's greatest collection of classic surfboards and also provides photo and art galleries displaying the legendary figures of surfing.

REGAL CINEMA. The Regal Cinema combines the architecture and ambience of Oceanside's earlier times with the modern technology required to provide customers with a state-of-the-art moviegoing experience.